Contents

How to use this book

How to use this book

This book forms the second part of a two part series which focuses on supporting children to develop working scientifically skills through 'child-led' enquiry activities.

Part 1 'Developing Young Scientists – a guide to child-led enquiry' outlines what is meant by child-led enquiry and contains 24 activities which support teachers with the experience, wonder, plan and investigate stages of the enquiry cycle see (figure 1). This book (part 2) focuses on what come after this: supporting children to review and explain what they have found out.

Figure 1: The enquiry cycle

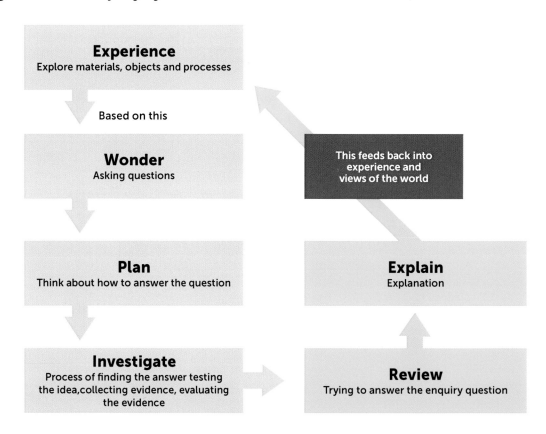

This book starts by discussing what children should record and highlights the importance of focused recording. The next sections outline how to support children in analysing data, drawing conclusions and making evaluations with age-appropriate examples across the year groups.

The final section will look at more creative ways that children can share their ideas in science. This could be used to inspire new approaches for science teaching and learning and the examples could also be used as an inspiration for children to then write their own versions.

Advice on what to record

What should children record?

A quick search of science investigation 'write up' results in numerous examples of worksheets which require children to complete boxes for all stages of an enquiry. Before embarking on using these, it is important to think about how well these support children in developing working scientifically skills.

Children should experience full enquiries to understand the complete process of generating questions and finding answers but there is no expectation for them to write up full investigations or 'scientific reports' and it is not part of the National Curriculum for children to learn to write a 'scientific report'. There are a range of working scientifically skills that children need to develop through enquiry such as recognising variables, recording results and drawing conclusions but trying to hit all of these areas in one enquiry is time consuming and may only result in shallow coverage. Children often find it tedious and onerous meaning the outcome does not necessarily showcase their understanding.

In contrast, focusing recording on a particular skill area such as drawing a conclusion, means there is more time for the 'doing' of the actual investigation, the vital discussion and the modelling of the particular skill. Recording in this way, also means that marking can be more focused on the development of a particular skill area.

Teachers often ask what skill or skills they should be focusing on. The answer to this depends on the coverage and assessment of skills up to that point. Across the range of scientific topics and enquiries, teachers need to ensure that all skills are covered in enough depth to be confident that the children have achieved these. It is also true that some enquiries lend themselves to coverage of certain skills better than others. For example, completing an enquiry into how the size of the parachute affects the time taken to fall is notoriously difficult to time. There is, therefore, a high chance that children may make mistakes in the timing leading to inaccurate results. For this reason, this a good enquiry to ask children to think carefully about the data and evaluate.

Planning advice

Many enquiry activities take more than one lesson, especially if they are child-led with the children taking more responsibility for the planning. For some schools, this may mean that there is potentially a gap of a week before they come back to the same enquiry. If this is the case, consider splitting the enquiry cycle so that the exploration, the wondering and planning are covered in one lesson and the hands on investigating and reviewing are carried out in the next. This means, that when the children are reviewing, the actual investigation is very fresh in their minds and this makes it easier for them to reflect on what they have done (which is particularly important for evaluations.)

Advice on what to record

Why this book focuses on developing conclusions and evaluations

When reviewing coverage of working scientifically skills, some schools find that conclusions and evaluations are the area which is most underdeveloped. In some cases this may be because they have always focused on recording all the stages of an enquiry. This means that, as conclusions and evaluations are at the end of the enquiry cycle, children may have run out of time, stamina and enthusiasm to really draw good conclusions and evaluations. Teachers also report that they often run out of time to fully cover this part of the enquiry cycle in the lesson time. This is an issue as the skills of analysing data, concluding and evaluating are demanding and require careful teaching and modelling. For this reason, the first two parts of this book are dedicated to carefully outlining what age appropriate conclusions and evaluations look like and supporting teachers in developing these.

Linking science with English and mathematics

Reviewing and communicating results from enquires also provides real-life, relevant contexts for children to apply their mathematical and English skills.

Analysing data and thinking more deeply about what it tells us and how much we can trust it, is a skill relevant to mathematics and science that some may argue is underdeveloped. For this reason, the *developing children's evaluations* section discusses how to encourage children to look more carefully at their data.

Science can also provide rich opportunities for writing across the genres including the more creative avenues such as poetry. For children to write confidently they need to know the science well so there are genuine benefits for both subjects in making strong and meaningful links. For this reason, the *getting creative in science recording* section focuses on how children can share their understanding through a variety of writing genres.

Types of enquiry – more than just fair testing

The term enquiry is used extensively throughout this book and it is important to remember that enquiry does not just refer to fair testing. There are five types of enquiry: fair/comparative testing, looking for a pattern, observing over time, identifying and classifying and research. It is a statutory requirement in the National Curriculum that children experience all five types of enquiry so it is important that all classroom teachers are aware of these and the differences between them.

In some case enquiries are being labelled as fair tests when they are actually one of the other types. It is, therefore, important to understand what the five types of enquiry are:

- **Fair and comparative testing** – changing **one** variable to observe its effect while controlling all of the other variables. e.g. **Which kitchen roll is most absorbent?**

Variable to change	type of kitchen roll
Variable to measure	how much water it will soak up
Variables to keep the same	volume of water it is placed in, size of the kitchen roll

To identify cause and effect children must change only one variable at a time.

- **Looking for patterns** – observing and recording patterns in nature or carrying out a survey where all of the variables cannot be controlled, e.g. where do daisies grow? Do children with the longest arms have the longest legs?

- **Research from secondary sources** – using books, the internet, pictures, visitors and experts as sources of evidence to answer questions.

- **Observing over time** – observing and measuring how something changes over time.

- **Identifying and classifying** – arranging and sorting objects, materials and livings things into particular sets according to certain characteristics. These can be characteristics and groups designed by the children or recognised groups such as carnivores, omnivores and herbivores.

Types of enquiry – more than just fair testing

This 'types of enquiry wheel' could be used as a reminder of the five different enquiry types that can be used to answer a science question.

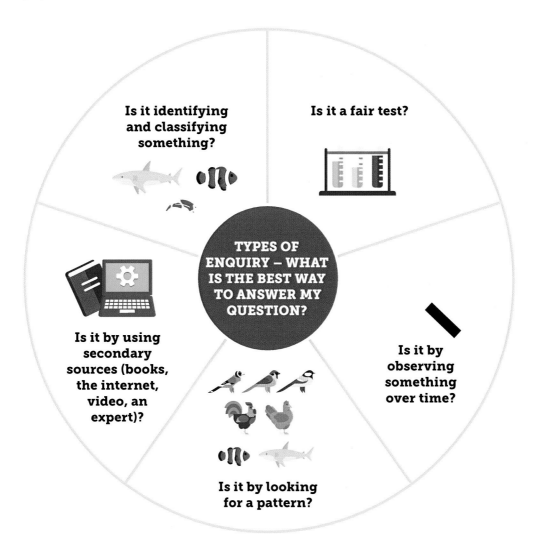

Summary points:

- There is no need for children to write up full investigations or scientific reports for every enquiry
- Focus recording on one or two skill areas that need to be developed and assessed
- Consider whether conclusions and evaluations need more focus
- Science can provide a rich context for children to apply English and mathematical skills
- Remember there are five types of enquiry

Developing children's conclusions

Forming a conclusion is an area that children often struggle with and some of their responses indicate that they do not know what a conclusion is.

Some common examples of what children say or write when asked to give a conclusion:

1) Stating whether the prediction was right or wrong:

> What are results were: /conclusion.
> Are results turned out exactly how we wanted it to be. Our bread with the Malt Vinegar followed our predictions

2) Identifying something as the 'best':

"the plastic was the best"

3) Repeating all of the results with no summary:

Water (40ml)	Time taken for colour to dissolve
hot	45 seconds
warm	1 min 40 seconds
cold	2 mins 20 seconds
sugar water (hot)	65 seconds

Developing children's conclusions

> **Our Conclusions** ✓
>
> The skittles took the least amount of time to dissolve in hot water which took 45 seconds, then it took the second least amount of time in sugar water which took 65 seconds, then warm water took the 2nd most amount of time of 1min 40 seconds then the skittles took the most amount of time to dissolve of 2 mins and 20 seconds in cold water. Next I would like to try to make a rainbow

Year 5 Pupil

Although certainly the first two examples may be a correct interpretation of the results, none of these responses are a clear conclusion which summarise what has been found out from the enquiry.

To improve on these types of responses, this section will tackle two key questions:

1) **What might a conclusion at each phase look like?**

2) **How do we teach children to form conclusions?**

Developing children's conclusions

What is a conclusion?

Dictionary definitions of the term conclusion include:

1) **a judgement or decision reached by reasoning**

2) **a summary of results**

These definitions are relatively useful for primary science as following an enquiry children need to to use their results and give a summary of what they have found out.

There are a number of working scientifically skills that are covered when children draw conclusions:

Phase	Relevant working scientifically skills*
KS1	• talks about their findings using everyday terms, text scaffolds or simple scientific language • with guidance begin to notice changes (i.e. cause and effect), patterns and relationships • talks about what they have found out and how they have found it out • **uses their observations and ideas to suggest answers to questions**
LKS2	• **reports on findings from enquiries, including oral and written explanations, displays or presentations of results and conclusions** • **uses results to draw simple conclusions** • **with support make predictions for new values and raise further questions** • with help, looks for changes, patterns, and relationships in their data • **uses straightforward scientific evidence to answer questions or to support their findings**
UKS2	• **reports on findings from enquiries**, using relevant scientific language and conventions, **in oral and written explanations such as displays and other presentations** • **identifies conclusions, causal relationships and patterns** • draws valid conclusions, explains and interprets the results **(including the degree of trust)** using scientific knowledge and understanding (e.g. recognises limitations of data)

*Note: Full lists of the working scientifically skills and tracking sheets can be found in HfL Primary PA Plus and the HfL Primary Science Package.

Developing children's conclusions

To help unpick the progression in conclusions and cover the relevant working scientifically skills it is useful to think about a conclusion as having **up to** three parts:

 **A basic summary**

 Use of data and observations

 Explanation

Developing children's conclusions

Part 1: A basic summary

The first part of a conclusion is a statement that clearly answers the original enquiry question. For example:

Enquiry question	Conclusion
Which paper towel is most absorbent?	Supermarket A was the most absorbent.
Which material muffles the sound most?	The wool muffled the sound the most.
How does the temperature affect the time taken to dissolve?	The hotter the water the quicker the sugar dissolved.
How does the size of the parachute affect the time taken to fall?	The bigger the parachute the longer it took to fall.
Do older children have bigger feet?	The older children generally had bigger feet.
Do seeds need soil to germinate?	The seeds did not need soil to germinate.

As this first part is an answer to the enquiry question, it is crucial that the question is of good quality. If the question is of a lower quality, (e.g. which is the best paper towel?), children will answer this question with: 'Supermarket A was the best.' This statement does not tell us quite as much about the child's learning, and what they have found out, as the example for this enquiry in the table above.

In KS2, this summary sentence is often a comparative sentence e.g.

*The **higher** the ramp the **further** the car travels.*

*The **hotter** the temperature the **quicker** the water evaporates.*

It may, therefore, be useful to remind children that they will need to write a comparative sentence (sometimes simply referred to as an 'er' 'er' sentence).

> **Top tip:** The first part of drawing a conclusion is about using observations and results to **answer the enquiry question**, therefore, make sure the question states specifically what the children are trying to find out.

Developing children's conclusions

Examples of a basic summary

Year 1	
Topic	Animals including humans
Enquiry question	What senses can we use to work out what the mystery foods are?

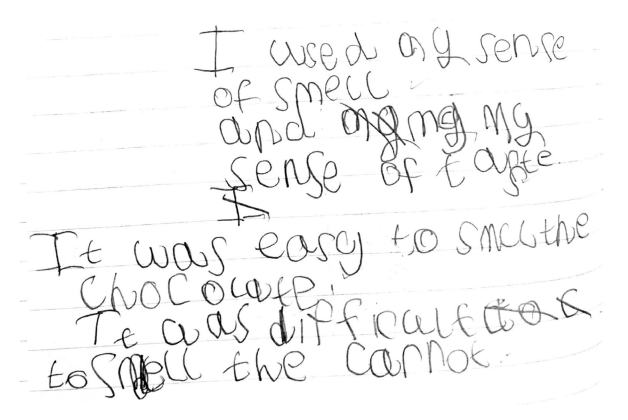

I used my sense of smell and my my sense of taste.

It was easy to smell the chocolate. It was difficult to smell the carrot.

Year 2	
Topic	Uses of everyday materials
Enquiry question	Which materials are waterproof?

Verbal conclusion: "We found out plastic is waterproof."

Developing children's conclusions

Year 3	
Topic	Forces and magnets
Enquiry question	Which materials will a magnet work though?

material	Prediction Does the magnet work through?	Actual
Paper cup	Y	Yes ✓
cardboard	N	Yes
cloth	Y	Yes
tissue paper	not sure	Yes

I found out that the magnet went through all the objects. ✓

Developing children's conclusions

Year 4	
Topic	Electricity
Enquiry question	Which materials conduct electricity?

Object	Prediction	conductor	insulator
balloon	conductor	✗	✓
coil	conductor	✓	✗
bulldog clip	conductor	✗ ✓	✓ ✗
casdle	insulator	✗	✓
Rock	insulator	✗	✓

1/16 I found out that balloons are made of metal rubber and I know rubber is an insul So, I now I, now know why the balloon didn't light the bub.

I have noticed that only metal makes the light bulb light up but that's only the metal I tried.

I'm suprised that Grapite, a typed of Rock is a conductor I also was suprised that cds an made of metal but coated in plastic.

The extra detail given by Luke is in this example reveals more understanding. It indicates that he is starting to think about the limitations of his data and conclusion when he says *'that's only the metal I tried.'*

Developing children's conclusions

Year 5	
Topic	Forces
Enquiry question	How does the size of the parachute affect the time taken to fall?

Question...	Does the size of the canopy affect the speed of the fall?		
	Parachute 1 (small canopy)	Parachute 2 (medium canopy)	Parachute 3 (large canopy)
Drop 1 (in seconds)	1.2	1.5	3.1
Drop 2 (in seconds)	1.3	1.9	3.6
Drop 3 (in seconds)	1.1	1.6	2.9
Average...	1.2 seconds	1.67 seconds	3.2 seconds

The results tell me that: _the smallest canopy took the quickest amount of time to fall and the greatest canopy took the longest time. So, the bigger the parachute, the longer it takes._

> Good examples of comparative sentences.

Year 6	
Topic	Electricity
Enquiry question	How does the number of bulbs in the circuit affect the brightness of the bulbs?

Light bulbs	brightness
1	really bright
2	a little bright
3	very dimly lit
4	extremely dim
5	doesn't work

Series circuit

I have come to conclude that when you add more bulbs in a series circuit each bulb gets dimmer. This means my prediction was correct because I thought the more bulbs added, the less current to power each bulb.*

r to ✓
diagrams

Developing children's conclusions

Useful questions to ask children to prompt a basic summary:

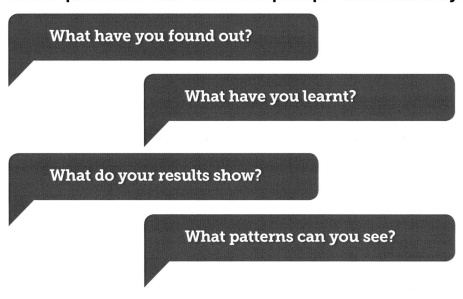

What have you found out?

What have you learnt?

What do your results show?

What patterns can you see?

Useful sentence starters:

I have found out...

My results show me that...

The pattern in my results...

Scaffold the response:

At times, it may also be appropriate to support children with learning how to make the comparative statement by modelling this and providing children with a sentence where they fill in the gaps:

I found out that the .... the parachute the .... the time it takes to fall to the floor.

Once they have learnt what it means to form a conclusion and make this comparative statement, this type of scaffolding can be taken away.

Part 2: Use of data and observations

The next step when forming a conclusion is for children to support their statement by saying **how** they know. This involves using results or observations to support the statement without repeating all of the results or observations. This is a challenging skill and not something that children often do naturally without prompting.

This skill first comes in at LKS2 where children are expected to 'use straightforward scientific evidence to answer questions or to support their findings.' In KS1 this is not something children need to do but asking them to explain 'how they know' often reveals more about their general understanding and embedding this expectation at any earlier stage will help the children as they move on.

It is also important to reflect on data at this point as it feeds into evaluation skills.

Examples of using data and observations

Year 1	
Topic	Animals including humans
Enquiry question	What colour eyes do we have in year 1?

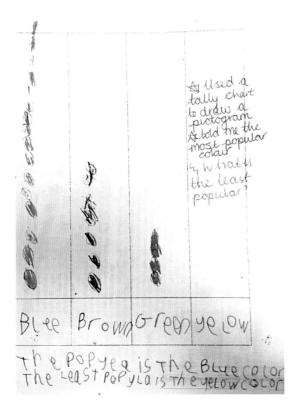

Example of a child using results/ data to answer questions.

In this example Ethan has written: *"The [most] pop[ular] is the blue colour. The least pop[ular] is the yellow colour."*

Developing children's conclusions

Year 2	
Topic	Use of everyday materials
Enquiry question	Which material should teddy choose for his rain coat?

Teddy should make his raincoat from

plastik *bag* ...

Because

it is the most water proofand it didst let us water drop in I didn't like real

In this example Emily has written: *"...it is the most waterproof and it didn't let any water drop in through the material."*

Emily has correctly identified which material was the most waterproof and used her observation to explain how they know this *'it didn't let any water drop in'.*

Year 2	
Topic	Animals including humans
Enquiry question	Are older children in Year 2 taller?

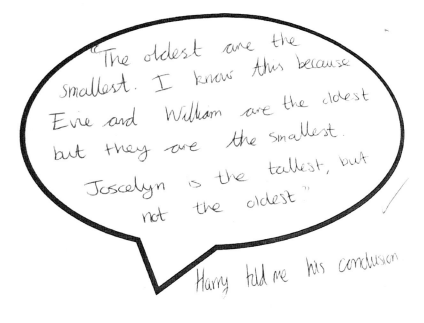

"The oldest are the smallest. I know this because Evie and William are the oldest but they are the smallest. Joscelyn is the tallest, but not the oldest"

Harry told me his conclusion

Developing children's conclusions

Year 2	
Topic	Use of everyday materials
Enquiry question	Which materials are waterproof?

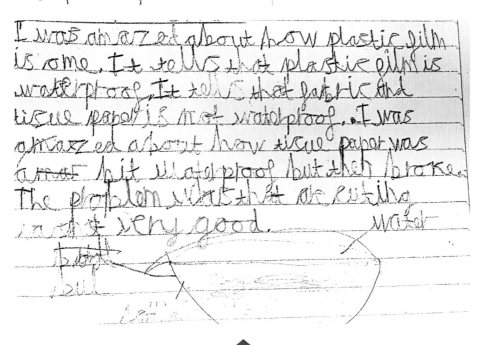

> *Daniel's teacher spoke to him and discovered that by 'ome' Daniel meant none.*

In this example Daniel has written: *"I was amazed about how plastic film is ome [none]. It tells that plastic film is waterproof. It tells that fabric and tissue paper is not waterproof. I was amazed about how tissue paper was a bit waterproof but then broke. The problem was that are cutting wasn't very good."*

In this example, Daniel has used the results to say what this tells him about the material and whether it is waterproof or not.

Developing children's conclusions

Year 3	
Topic	Rocks
Enquiry question	What type of soil is most permeable? (This group of children measured how much water passed through the soil in 30 seconds.)

Result

A	150ml
B	250ml
C	190ml

Conclusion

1

I found out. that soil B was the most permeable. I guessed soil B would be the most permeable because it had only an inch of sand at the bottom and lot's of top soil. I found out that, in each cup of soil there we more then 100 ml of water. that had passed through. Something strange was that soil A had less water then soil B which had the rock in it. This is because there was a big gap so all the water could go through.

In this example, Evie is starting to use her results and observations to support her conclusion.

Developing children's conclusions

Year 4	
Topic	Sound
Enquiry question	How does the amount of water in the bottle affect the pitch of the sound?

What did you find out?

I found out that is there is lots of water it is high pitch and is there is less water it is low pitch

5cm, 11.5cm, 15cm and 19cm are low and 25cm is high pitch.

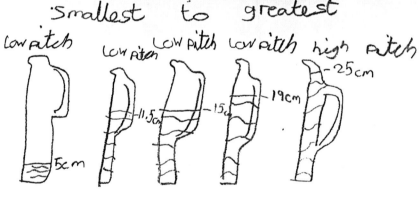

Smallest to greatest

low pitch   low pitch   low pitch   low pitch   high pitch

5cm   11.5cm   15cm   19cm   25cm

To encourage Alfie to think a bit further, it would be good to ask Alfie if he noticed any difference in the pitch when 5cm of water was used and 15cm of water was used.

Year 5	
Topic	Properties and changes of materials
Enquiry question	How does the temperature of the water affect the time a skittle takes to dissolve?

We found out that the hotter the water the quicker the skittle dissolved. I know this because when we did the cold water which was 20℃ it took 2 minutes and 10 second but when I put the hot water which was 40°C it only took 30 seconds.

I think if we used the hotter water it would dissolve even quicker.

Developing children's conclusions

Year 6	
Topic	Evolution and inheritance
Enquiry question	Which tool will pick up the most seeds in a minute?

Food types	Peg	Scissors	Spoon	Lolly sticks	Straws
Rice	15 grains	88 grains	774 grains	67 grains	6 grains
Marbles	7 marbles	0 marbles	48 marbles	13 marbles	0 marbles
Water	10 ml	3 ml	71 ml	3 ml	1 ml
Bird food	5 seeds	54 seeds	102 seeds	77 seeds	17 seeds
counters	7 counters	16 counters	72 counters	10 counters	0 counters
dried peas	3 peas	8 peas	35 peas	98 peas	5 peas

Conclusion!

The spoon was the best beak to eat up all the types of food. It ate the highest food intake was rice with 774 grains. So the answer to the question & which beak is the best adapted for all the food the answer is a spoon. And the straw was the worst.

In this example Lizzy has written:
"The spoon was the best beak to eat up all the types of food. Its highest food intake was rice with 774 grains. So the answer to the question which beak is best adapted for all the food the answer is a spoon. And the straw was the worst."

In the example above, Lizzy has used one result to support her statement. The teacher then worked with Lizzy's group and together they wrote a better conclusion:

"The spoon was the most effective tool for picking up all of the food items as it picked up the highest amount in every case. For the bird seed, on average the spoon picked up 102 seeds which was more than double what the scissors picked up and 35 seeds more than the lollysticks (the second most effective)."

Note: in this enquiry the children have changed two variables: the type of tool, and the type of food. It is recommended that children only change one variable as it is easier to then draw a conclusion.

Developing children's conclusions

Useful questions to encourage children to use results to support their statements:

> How do you know this?

> What evidence do you have to support this?

> Can you use your results to support this statement?

Useful sentence starters:

> I know this because...

> The highest/quickest... whereas

It is also useful for teachers to model how to use their observations and data perhaps through drawing class conclusions that use results to support the summary statement.

To encourage the children to think more deeply about their data and results they could also be asked:

- What do you think would happen if....... (you used hotter water, more water, a different tool etc)?
- Do you think this pattern will carry on?
- Looking at your results, is there anything else you would like to investigate?

Developing children's conclusions

Part 3: Explanation

The third part of a conclusion involves children linking what they have found out to scientific understanding as they explain why they think something has happened. However, it is not always appropriate to ask children to do this. There are occasions in primary science where the knowledge required for an explanation goes beyond the knowledge children are expected to acquire in KS1 or KS2. This means it is **not always possible for children to explain why something has happened**. Examples of this include:

Year 2 Materials

In year 2, children investigate properties of materials and find out which materials are waterproof. They might make generalisations and realise that different types of plastic are waterproof but it is not expected that they would be able to say why this is the case.

Year 4 Electricity

In year 4, after investigating which materials are conductors a pupil might say I have found out that all metals are conductors. Asking them to explain why this happens would require understanding of why metals conduct (knowledge not expected until KS4).

Year 5 Properties and changes of materials

In year 5, children investigate the effect of temperature on dissolving to find out that the hotter the water the quicker something dissolves. Asking them to explain why this happens would require understanding of particles and energy (KS3 knowledge).

There are, however, enquiries where asking children to try and explain why they think something happens extends and reveals more about their scientific understanding. It also often requires them to use key vocabulary.

Examples of appropriate explanations

Year 2	
Topic	Plants
Enquiry question	What are the conditions needed for a seed to germinate?

Some of the comments from the children after the enquiry included:

> "I was surprised that it germinated with no soil. It has made me think that seed don't need soil to germinate."

In response to why a seed germinated in the dark:

> "Maybe it is because seeds are normally underground so they don't need light to germinate."

Year 3	
Topic	Forces and magnets
Enquiry question	What force does it take to move different shoes?

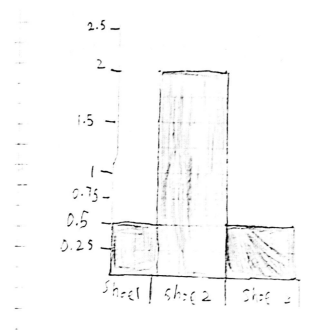

In this example, Jake has written:

"Shoe 1 has square designed soles. It took 0N of force to make it move. This is because the square designed soles makes less friction between the shoe and the bench.

Shoe 2 has leopard print sole. It took 2N of force to make it move. This is because the leopard print sole makes more friction."

Please note: Although he has correctly said that a shoe is easier to move when there is less friction, James has incorrectly stated that it took 0N to move John's shoe. This mistake would need to be discussed with James. He also needs support with drawing a scale on the x axis of the graph.

Developing children's conclusions

Year 5	
Topic	Forces
Enquiry question	How does the shape of plasticine affect the time taken to fall through water?

Shapes	1st	2nd	3rd	Average
circle	0.6 0.72s 0.34		0.65	1.71s
sausage	0.34 s	0.53s	0.25s	0.37s
Pancake	0.62s	0.65s	0.68s	0.65s

Conclusion:

The sausage was the the quickest to travel through water because it was *streamline. The slowest was the circle because it had a large surface area. My prediction was that the sausage would be the quickest and my prediction was correct.

Water resistance is agg effected by the shape and weight of an object. If you had a peice of blue tack that was thin and one flat the thin one would get down quicker because it would be in a streamlined position and the flat one would be slow because it would have a large surface area which would make it slow down.

In this example, Emma shows good understanding of the terms *'streamline'* and *'water resistance'.*

Unfortunately, the mean has been calculated incorrectly for the circle. Emma has made a common mistake: she has added the times correctly but forgotten to divide by three. Asking Emma to look closely at the data to support her statement might have resulted in her picking up this mistake and then she would have been able to correct her conclusion. This shows how important it is to ask children to use their data to support their statements.

Developing children's conclusions

Year 6	
Topic	Animals including humans
Enquiry question	How does exercise affect my pulse rate?

Resting heart rate

Beats in 15 Seconds	Beats per minutes	Mean
17	68	
19	76	
15	60	65
15	60	
15	60.	

My resting heart rate mode is 60 beats per minute.

Vigorous heart rate

Beats in 15 seconds	Beats per minute	Mean
39	159	
36	144	154
39	159	

My mode is 159 beats per minute. It is faster because when i'm running my body needs more oxygen. So my heart pumps faster.

A simple and clear explanation that shows good understanding about the job of the heart.

Developing children's conclusions

Useful questions to encourage children to think about an explanation:

> Can you link what we have been learning to what you have found out?

> Is there anything you know that might explain why this happened?

> What do these results tell you about... (plants, forces, yeast etc.)?

Summary

By the end of KS2 a complete conclusion may have **up to** three parts:

1) A basic summary
2) Use of data and observations
3) Explanation

Before asking children to explain, encourage them to use their data to support their statement. This helps them to think carefully about whether the conclusion they are making is right. It is also helps them to spot any errors and will help them with the skill of evaluating.

Remember children might not always be able to explain what they have found out as the knowledge may go beyond the primary curriculum.

Developing children's conclusions

Examples of good conclusions from each group

Year 1	
Topic	Animals including humans
Enquiry question	What is the eye colour and hair colour in year 1?

The teacher asked the children what they had found out and these are their responses:

"More people have blue eyes in Year 1"

"More people have brown hair"

"Not many people have red hair in our class"

Year 2	
Topic	Uses of everyday materials
Enquiry question	What is the most waterproof material to make Teddy's coat from?

Teddy should make his raincoat from

plastik *bactyrial*

Because

it is the most
water proof and
it did'nt let in
water drop in
troou the
matirial

In this example Emily has written: *"...it is the most waterproof and it didn't let any water drop in through the material."*

Emily has correctly identified which material was the most waterproof and used her observation to explain how they know this *'it didn't let any water drop in'*.

Developing children's conclusions

Year 3	
Topic	Forces
Enquiry question	How does the surface affect the distance a car will travel?

<u>Results</u>

Material	1st attempt	2nd attempt	3rd attempt	Average
plastic	2m 21cm	2m 30cm	2m 76cm	2.46m
Wooden floor	1.95cm 3cm	1.16cm	1m	1.0m
foil	72cm	82cm	64cm	0.72cm

Model conclusion for these results:

"The car travelled the furthest on the plastic – over 2 metres. It travelled the least far on the foil. This is because the wooden floor creates low friction as its smooth and the bumpy foil creates high friction."

Year 4	
Topic	Sound
Enquiry question	How do you get high and low pitch from the pipes?

<u>Pan Pipes</u>

How do you get high and low pitch different Sound from the pipes? and how could it affect it?

It's that the shorter the pipe is the higher pitch it would make but the longer it is the lower the pitch would be, because they is more place to vibrate but with the shorter ones theys less place to vibrate.

C D E F high
G high
high
low

Developing children's conclusions

Year 5	
Topic	Properties and changes of materials
Enquiry question	How does the temperature of the water affect the time a skittle takes to dissolve?

We found out that the hotter the water the quicker the skittle dissolved. I know this because when we did the cold water which was 20°C it took 2 minutes and 10 seconds but when I put the hot water which was 40°C it only took 30 seconds.

I think if we used the hotter water it would dissolve even quicker.

In this example, Mia has drawn a valid conclusion and used evidence to support this. She has also made a prediction about the results beyond the data collected. The explanation for how this happens is above the knowledge expected at KS2.

Year 6	
Topic	Electricity
Enquiry question	How does the number of bulbs in the circuit affect the brightness of the bulb?

Year 6 electricity investigation

Number of bulbs	Brightness
1	3300 lux
2	1250 Lux, 1190 lux
3	885lux, 870 lux, 900lux

I found out that the more bulbs added to the circuit the dimmer they will be. It is quite a big difference as one bulb had 3300 lux, whereas when there were three bulbs the average lux was 885 lux (under half the brightness). I think if I added another bulb they would be so dim that it would be hard to see the light.

I think the bulbs get dimmer when more are in the circuit as the battery has to power more bulbs so the strength of the battery has to be shared.

I would like to find out what happens to the loudness of a buzzer if we add more. I think they will get quieter when there are more in a circuit.

In this example, Hannah has summarised the results to draw a conclusion and used results to support her statement. She has predicted what would happen if she were to extend the investigation by adding another bulb and she has thought of another enquiry question. The knowledge required to fully explain why the bulbs get dimmer goes beyond KS2 understanding but she has made a good attempt at giving an explanation.

Developing children's evaluations

Getting children to evaluate is perhaps even harder than drawing conclusions. However, when teachers encourage children to use their results or data to support their conclusions (as described in the previous section) it is then not such a huge step to get them to think about the quality of their data and how much they can trust it. From this, teachers can then encourage children to reflect on the method and how this could be improved. This is why the skills of concluding and evaluating often go hand in hand.

As with drawing conclusion, the expectations for evaluations increase throughout the key stages:

Phase	Relevant working scientifically skills*
KS1	• with support, suggests whether or not what happened was what they expected • with support, suggest different ways they could have done things
LKS2	• with support, uses results to **suggest improvements** to what they have done
UKS2	• reports on the **degree of trust** in their results. Makes practical suggestions about how their working method could be improved

*Note: Full lists of the working scientifically skills and tracking sheets can be found in HfL Primary PA Plus and the HfL Primary Science Package.

Supporting children to reflect on their results and evaluate

When starting to evaluate an investigation children often start to comment on factors such as how well they worked together. Just like drawing conclusions the skill of evaluating needs to be explicitly taught and modelled.

Supporting children in KS1

In KS1, children start evaluating by thinking about whether what happened is what they expected. With support, they also need to think about things they could do differently.

It is not too hard at this age for children to be surprised by results as they often have misconceptions and incorrect ideas about how things work.

Developing children's evaluations

Useful questions to ask KS1 children when reflecting on results:

> What were you surprised by?

> What were you amazed by?

> Does anyone have any other ideas of how we could test...?

> Does anyone have any other ideas of how we could measure...?

Example from Year 1	
Topic	Materials
Enquiry question	Which materials will float?

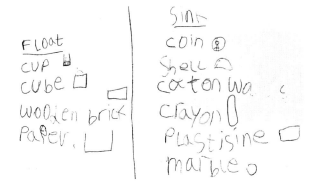

The teacher asked the children to reflect on what they were surprised by and encouraged them to use the word *because* in their answers.

The children said:

> "I was surprised the wooden brick floated because wood is strong."

> "I was surprised the cotton wool sink because it is light and fluffy."

In further discussion one child then said:

> "I think we should leave the paper to see if it sink."

Supporting children in KS2

As discussed in the previous section, in KS2, children are expected to begin to use their results and observations to support their findings. In terms of evaluating, in UKS2 they also need to think about the *'degree of trust'* they have in their results, why they might not trust them and what improvements they could make if they were to repeat the investigation.

There are certain enquiries that often produce results and data where the degree of trust can be questioned and a perfect example of this is when children investigate parachutes.

Year 5	
Topic	Forces
Enquiry question	How does the shape of the parachute affect the time taken to fall?

Shape of the parachute	Attempt 1 and time	Attempt 2 and time	Attempt 3 and time
triangle	3 secs	1 secs	2 secs
star	1 secs	2 secs	1 secs
hexagon	4 secs	1 secs	4 secs

The children went on to conclude that the hexagon shape took the longest to fall, which is what the data would suggest. However, it could be argued that this data could be questioned as there is considerable overlap in the times recorded for the different shapes.

This is, therefore, a great opportunity to ask children a series of questions to get them to reflect on how much they trust their data.

Developing children's evaluations

Suggested questions:

> How confident are you in your results?

> Are there any odd results?

> Are there any results that do not follow the pattern?

> Why do you think these results might be odd? (This might prompt the children to think about their method and any errors they made)

Finally thinking about their answers to the above questions they could then answer:

> How confident are you in your conclusion?

Here are another set of results for the parachute enquiry which would be appropriate to question and reflect on.

Year 5	
Topic	Forces
Enquiry question	How does the size of the parachute affect the time taken to fall?

Size of Parachute (cm)	Test - 1	Test - 2	Test - 3
30 × 30 Square	1.08	1.00	1.09
15 × 15 square	0.50	0.65	0.57
6 × 6 square	0.62	0.64	0.59

If this child was to calculate the mean, they would find that the mean times are:

- 0.62 seconds for the 6x6 parachute size
- 0.57 seconds for the 15x15 parachute size

This is not what is expected and, in this case, children need to use their understanding of science to question the data as they predicted that the larger the parachute size the longer it will take to fall and this is certainly the case for the 30 x 30 parachute.

It is often the case, that results for this investigation need to be questioned, as because of the very small differences in the time taken to fall, there is a high probability that mistakes will be made with timing.

Developing children's evaluations

In this case, and other examples like this, useful questions to ask the children include:

Do you think you made any mistakes in your investigation?

How accurate do you think you were when timing or measuring?

Do you have enough data to be confident in your conclusion?

Do you trust your data?

What could you do to be more confident in your data?

Was there anything that would have affected your results that you should have controlled but did not?

Developing children's evaluations

Examples of evaluations

Year 4	
Topic	Sound
Enquiry question	Does sound travel further from a larger megaphone?

	Distance
Large megaphone	59 m
Small megaphone	54 m

My results show me that the large megapho me makes sound travel gurtter than the Small mega phone. I & I were to do this again again, I might think about going to a quiet place with kno backround noise so I could do it properley. Consider that during my gist the large megaphode, there were lots of other groups doing theirs at the same time and this may have affected the result.

(the large one)

In this example, Caitlyn has identified that the background noise might have affected the results and given a suggestion about how to improve this.

Developing children's evaluations

Year 5	
Topic	Animals including humans
Enquiry question	How does length of finger affect the distance a ball of paper can be flicked?

In our investigation, we weren't able to find any link between the length of fingers and the distance of the ball flick.

For example, there was a finger length of 7cm and the average flicked was 25cm, finger length of 5.7cm and the average flicked was 2m, finger length of 6cm and the average flicked was 261cm.

It might not have been a fair test because some people me could have flicked it but then it bounced off of the table or someone. To cheat, they might have pushed the paper ball with their hand or their fist. Some might have flicked it from over the line, whereas some might have put it far too back from the line. Although Although we had results finished results, some of them will must not be true at all

In this example,
Lily has correctly
concluded
that there
seems to be no
relationship
between length
of finger and
the distance of
the ball flick and
used results to
support this.

She has then
gone on to
describe some
of the factors
that might have
affected how
far each ball
was flicked.

In this example Lily has written: *"In our investigation, we weren't able to find any link between the length of fingers and the distance of ball flick.*

For example, there was a finger length of 7cm and the average flicked was 25cm, another finger length of 5.7cm and the average flicked was 2m, finger length of 6cm and the average flicked was 261cm.

It might not have been a fair test because some people could have flicked it but then it bounced off the table or someone. To cheat, they might have pushed the paper ball with their hand or their first. Some might have flicked it from over the line, whereas, some might have put it too far back from the line. Although we finished results, some of them must not have been true."

Please note: this enquiry is not possible to make a *'fair test'* as there are variables which cannot be controlled. It is therefore a *'looking for a pattern'* enquiry.

Developing children's evaluations

A whole school enquiry to teach the skill of evaluation

As mentioned in the introduction, there are some enquiries which lend themselves more readily to evaluation than others.

A great enquiry for teaching the skill of evaluation which could be run in any year group is:

Do bigger hands grab more sweets?

Children could be given more responsibility for working out how to answer this question to make the planning more child-led. However, as this enquiry is being used to develop and focus on the skills of evaluation, instructions are given below for children to follow. This means there are points for improvement which are easy for children to identify.

1. Show children how to measure hand span which is the distance between the thumb and little finger on an out stretched hand. Children measure and record hand span.

2. Give each table a selection of different sized wrapped sweets (see picture) and make sure some tables have more than others (this will lead to some points of discussion in the evaluation). Children take it in turn to grabs as many sweets as possible in one grab, count how many and record the results.

3. Ask children to look at the results for everyone in their group and try to look for any patterns.

Developing children's evaluations

After children have started to think about whether there is a pattern in their data, gather data for the whole class and talk about why it is useful to have more data when looking for a pattern.

Results from a Year 6 class

Hand span (cm)	Number of sweets
12	8, 12, 14
13	13, 9,
14	11, 14, 12, 9
15	9, 16, 15, 15, 10
16	8, 11, 9, 13, 14
17	17, 19,
18	15, 11
19	14, 9
20	11

A key teaching point is that to spot a pattern it is useful to put the hand spans in order of smallest to biggest (this is not something children normally do without prompting).

As you can see from the table above, there is often no pattern in the data. This could be because there is no relationship between hand span and the number of sweets we can grab. However, in the original method there were several factors that may also have meant that some children were able to grab more or less sweets. There are, therefore, several improvements that could be made to the method to improve the quality of the results.

To encourage children to identify these problems with the method, ask them to think about:

- Is there a pattern in the results?
- Why might there be no pattern in the results?
- How good was your method at answering the enquiry question?
- Was there anything you should have controlled that might have affected the number of sweets grabbed?

Developing children's evaluations

The element of competition and the clear differences in the sweets given to each table or group and how they grab, means children come up with some good suggestions of things that might have affected the results. Examples include:

> "Some sweets were smaller than others and easier to grab."

> "That table had a bigger pile of sweets so they will have been able to grab more."

> "Some people piled up the sweets before they grabbed them so they were able to get more."

Some children also begin to ask questions such as:

> "Does it matter if someone used their left hand or right hand?"

> "Does the shape of the sweet matter?"

These children have all identified problems with the initial method that will affect the results. They are also relatively easy things for children to control if they were to repeat the investigation.

e.g. use 20 Chewits, on a paper plate, evenly spread out and everyone grab with the hand you write with.

If time is not a limitation it would be good to give children time to discuss how they will improve the method before giving them the time to complete the investigation again and then compare the results.

Note: Do bigger hands grab more sweets? This enquiry is a *'looking for a pattern'* enquiry not a *'fair test'*. However, when completing a *'looking for a pattern'* enquiry children can still think about factors or variables that they need to control or keep the same. This is any variable that might affect the results which, in this case, is the number of sweets grabbed.

Summary

Some enquires and set of results lend themselves more readily to the skills of evaluation.

To support children in evaluating it is important to ask them key probing questions which get them to reflect on not only what they did but also the quality of their results.

Traditional methods of presenting and reporting

At each phase, children are expected to present and report on findings.

Expectations for reporting on findings:

Phase	Relevant working scientifically skills*
KS1	• with help, they should record and communicate their findings in a range of ways and begin to use simple scientific language
LKS2	• records and presents findings using drawings, labelled diagrams, keys, tally charts, Carroll diagrams, Venn diagrams, bar charts and tables • reporting on findings from enquiries, including oral and written explanations, displays or presentations of results and conclusions
UKS2	• records and presents findings using scientific diagrams and labels, classification keys, tables, scatter graphs, bar and line graphs • reports on findings from enquiries in simple scientific language, using oral and written explanations, displays or presentations of results and conclusions

*Note: full lists of the working scientifically skills and tracking sheets can be found in HfL Primary PA Plus and the HfL Primary Science Package.

This section will provide some quick tips and ideas for supporting children in using tables, Venn diagrams, Caroll diagrams and graphs.

Tables and graphs: a few quick tips

Children sometimes forget the tally chart is often one of the simplest ways to organise results.

Type of insect	Amount Seen
bee		
butterfly	
fly	
Hover fly	
Ladybug	
Other	

Another key point that children need to be reminded of, is that results tables are clearer when the columns have titles:

Liquid name	Time it took to ... down tray
water	0.44s
Ketchup	5mt
syrup	19.78s ! What ... y
salad cream	5mt → informati
oil	1.46s

Although children do need to draw their own results tables, it may be appropriate to provide a template if the table is difficult to construct:

Material of the parachute	Time taken to fall (seconds)			
	1st attempt	2nd attempt	3rd attempt	mean

Drawing graphs

There are two important questions to ask before setting children the task of representing their data in a graph:

1) Does this graph help to interpret the data?

This is important as, if the table or tally chart can easily be used to answer the enquiry question and reflect on the data, a graph might not be necessary. Drawing a graph is far more meaningful for children if it helps them to spot a pattern.

2) Is this an age appropriate graph to draw in terms of mathematical skills?

If a class wanted to find out whether the taller children have bigger feet, the graph needed to represent this data is a scatter graph. However, the skill of drawing a scatter graph is not covered in the mathematics curriculum until KS3. It is therefore appropriate to think about how to support children with representing data in this way through perhaps drawing a whole class graph or providing a template.

A good example of where drawing the graph helps with interpreting results:

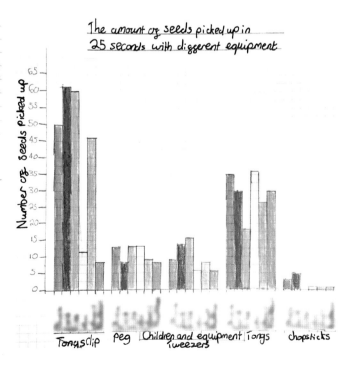

Example of a class graph in Year 2:

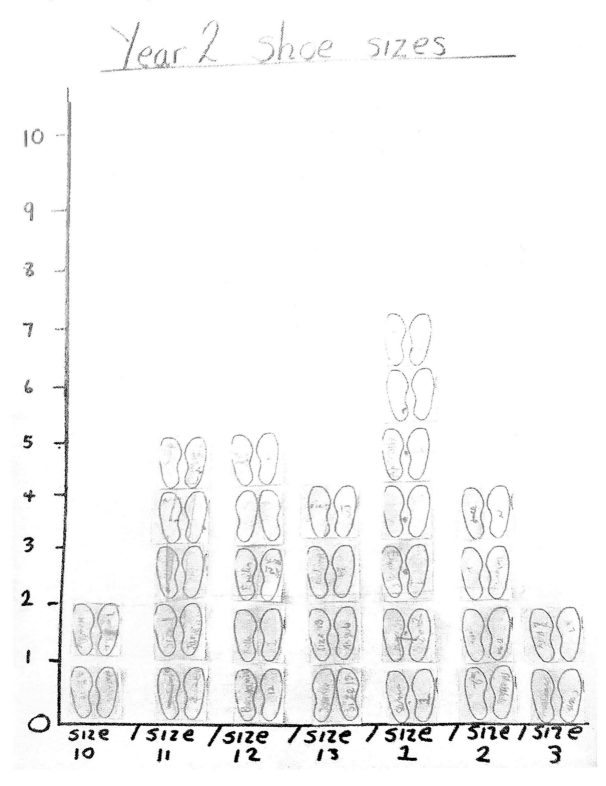

Venn diagrams, sorting circles and Caroll diagrams

Sorting circles can be used to record predictions, results and for classification like in the examples below.

Examples of using sorting circles

Year 1	
Topic	Materials
Enquiry question	Which objects will float or sink?

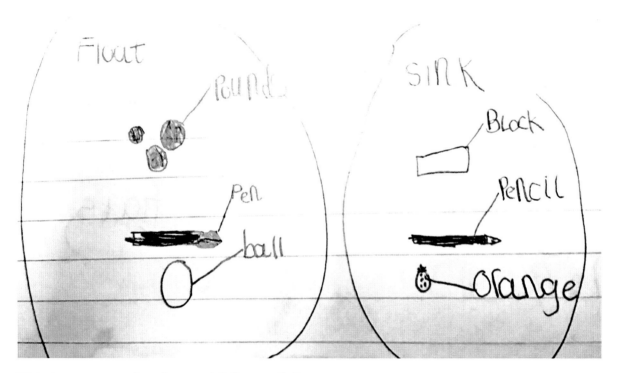

This is an example of one child's predictions.

Year 1	
Topic	Plants
Enquiry question	What parts of the plant can we eat?

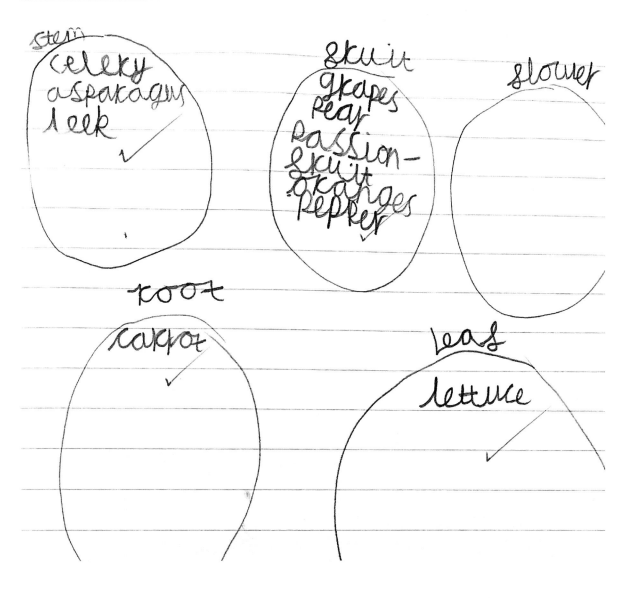

Venn diagrams and Carroll diagrams are also great for *identification and classification* enquiries and comparison. Children can be given headings or come up with their own.

Examples of Venn and Carroll diagrams

Year 1	
Topic	Animals including humans
Enquiry question	What are the diets of different animals?

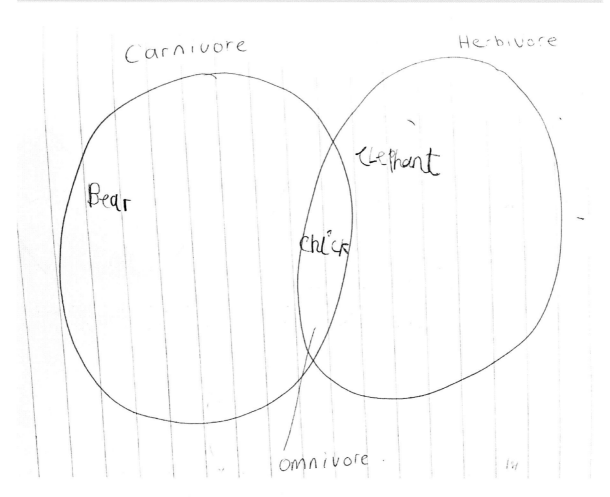

Year 4	
Topic	Living things and their habitats
Enquiry question	How can you group these animals? (the children came up with their own groups).

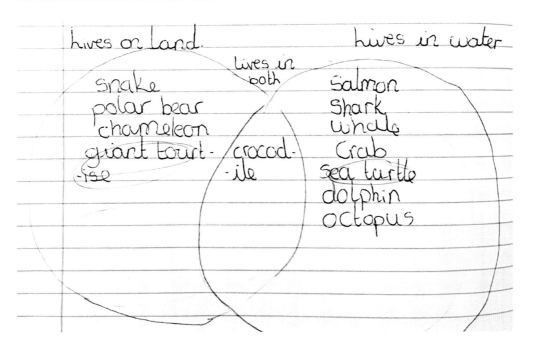

Year 6	
Topic	Evolution and inheritance
Enquiry question	What characteristics are inherited or due to the environment or both? (Children completed research and then decided how to record what they had found out).

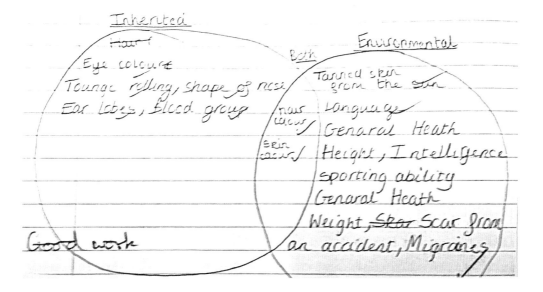

Traditional methods of presenting and reporting

	Legs	No legs
Pet		
Wild animal		

When children are familiar with these different approaches for recording and presenting their answers or scientific understanding, they can be asked to choose the method they would like to use to clearly show their understanding.

Year 2	
Topic	Animals including humans
Enquiry question	How can we use a Carroll diagram to group animals?

Now for the real fun part!

Sharing understanding in science can be really fun and engaging whilst providing a great context for writing across the genres. This section will explore a range of strategies that can be used to do just this. It is not an exhaustive list but it is hoped the ideas will develop science teaching and learning and spark further creative ideas.

For each strategy there will be examples from children with comments about the evidence this shows in terms of the child's understanding. There will also be a few suggestions of other contexts where these strategies could be used. These ideas could be shared in staff meetings or at joint planning sessions to develop further contexts that they could be used in to make science recording more varied and engaging. The examples may also be useful to begin moderation discussions.

Ideas in this section include:

1. Annotated diagrams and cartoon strips
2. Poetry
3. Recount
4. Documentaries and script writing
5. Newspaper report
6. Letter writing
7. Instructions

Getting creative with science recording

Annotated diagrams and cartoon strips

An annotated diagram can often tell us a lot about a child's understanding.

Year 4	
Topic	Sound

The class were exploring how to change the pitch and volume on a number of 'home-made' instruments. They were encouraged to draw labelled diagrams to show what they noticed.

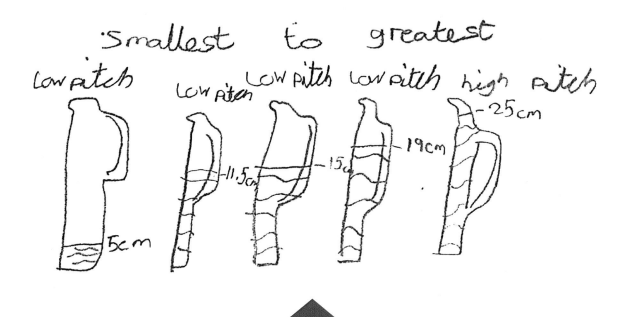

In this example, Alfie has shown what happens to the pitch as he added more water and blew across the bottle. This shows he has understood the term pitch and is starting to think about how it changes.

It would be interesting to ask him if there was any difference in the pitch when 5cm of water was used and the pitch when 15 cm of water was used.

Getting creative with science recording

To take the idea of labelled drawings a step further children could draw cartoon strips.

Year 5	
Topic	Properties and changes of materials

The class have been exploring dissolving sugar in water and tea and the teachers asked the class to show what happens to the sugar in a cartoon strip.

This example shows that Lauren has understood that the sugar cannot be seen after it has dissolved and that it has not melted. The teacher has decided to check her understanding by asking her to explain how we know the sugar is still there which is appropriate as it is not clear at this point whether she understands this.

Lauren went on to say that you can taste the sugar and with further prompting said that you can evaporate the water to leave just the sugar behind in the cup. This indicates good understanding of dissolving.

Getting creative with science recording

Year 6	
Topic	Living things and their habitat

The class had been learning about microorganisms and harmful microorganisms which can cause disease. The teacher introduced them to historical ideas on disease and the fact that at one point in history doctors would not wash their hands. The class talked about the work of Ignaz Semmelweis who was the first to suggest that doctors should wash hands between patients. After completing some further individual research, the children created story boards or comic strips to show their learning.

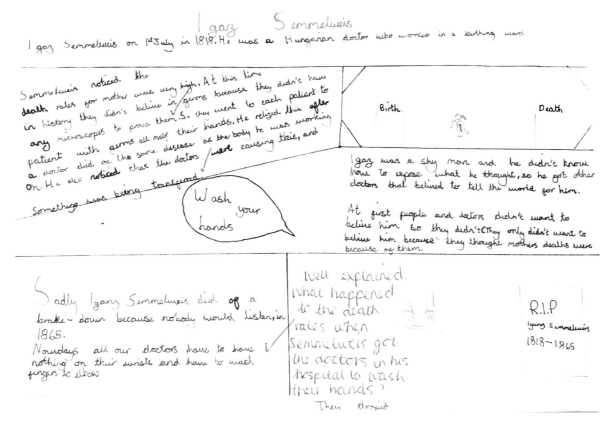

The National Curriculum has a range of relevant scientists the children could research and then create story boards or cartoon strips about including: Mary Anning, Charles Darwin and Jane Goodhall.

Other contexts children could use cartoon strips to share their understanding:

- Cartoon strip to show the investigation and the outcome of an enquiry (This can be done using pictures if children take pictures during the investigation, for example the 'Dunking biscuits' enquiry from part 1.)

- Cartoon strip to outline the work of a famous scientist

- Cartoon strip to the show the journey of something e.g. Journey of a red blood cell (Year 6), journey of water droplet (Year 4) or journey of a sandwich (Year 4)

Poetry

This is not often a type of writing which teachers expect to see in science books but it can be a powerful way to develop the use of vocabulary and share understanding.

Year 4	
Topic	Animals including humans

After several lessons learning about digestion, children were challenged to either make interactive posters or write a poem to show what they had learned. Mark chose to write a poem.

Mark's Pizza

Hello, I am Mark's pizza,
And I must say it's nice to meet ya!
Now I am going into his mouth,
And when I am finished, I will be smaller than a mouse.
Where am I? It is really dark.
I hope that this won't leave mark.
Goodness, I think I'll be as small as sand.
Could someone please hold my hand?
I know I don't have one, but this is very strange!
That I am going down in this sort of range.
Now I am in the oesophagus, I am going through so much!
There is so many things of such.
I am in the stomach, something is making me spin!
I can't run nor can I swim!
I am lastly in the small intestine.
There aint no time for resting!
Goodbye kids, have some fun!
This is what your food will be like – they feel like they've been stunned!

In this poem, Mark has identified some of the organs in the digestive system (mouth, oesophagus, stomach and small intestine). It shows that he understands the order food moves through these four parts and he is hinting at one of the actions of the stomach when he says it makes him spin. It is also clear that he understands that digestion breaks food down.

There are a few questions to ask Mark to check he fully understands digestion:

• What happens in the small intestine?

• Why food is broken down?

• What happens after the small intestine?

He could be encouraged to add extra detail but as he has clearly put effort into making the poem rhyme it might be better to do this through discussion.

Year 6	
Topic	Animals including humans

After lessons to build a good understanding of the heart and its role within the circulatory system, children were challenged to write poems focusing on how important it is.

In this example Haleem has written *"Caged in bone,*
this muscle is the epicentre,
to our lives,
the on going galloping,
is uncontrolable,
at it expands and contracts,
its is an energizer
a life provider
When it beats
it is like a punch
thrusting the life giving fluid
round our magical body"

In this example, Haleem, has shown that he knows that the purpose of the heart is to pump blood around the body. (From discussions it was clear that he was referring to blood). The adjectives and figurative language create a powerful picture of the heart and his teacher was able to infer a lot about his science understanding. There are some questions we could ask Haleem to clarify some of the points in the poem and his understanding of the circulatory system:

• Why have you described the heart as an energizer and life provider?

• What does the blood transport around the body?

• Where does the oxygen come from?

Getting creative with science recording

Other examples of where children could write poems to share understanding:

- To outline the seasons in seasonal change in Year 1

- After completing research on the solar system in Year 5 earth and space

- After exploring solids, liquids and gases and their properties in Year 4

- After making and exploring cornflour gloop
  (This can be done when exploring properties of materials in KS1 or specifically exploring the properties of solids, liquids and gases in KS2. Children would need to make close observations of the material and what it is like.)

- After making close observations of something in nature (seed, flower, daffodil etc.)

Getting creative with science recording

Recount

There are lots of opportunities for children to write recounts in science. To show science understanding these will need to include key vocabulary and explain certain information that the children have learnt. The recounts often cover stages in a process so it may be useful for children to use story maps or create a flow diagram so they know what their recount should include.

As well as producing writing which is informative, children can also be encouraged to think about the reader and make their recount entertaining or playful by using imagination. Some children become immersed in this idea often creating personalities to tell the story and engage the reader.

Year 2	
Topic	Plants

The class investigated seeds germinating by making observations over time and studied the text of *'The Tiny Seed'* by Eric Carle. In English, they were set the tasks of planning and then writing a diary from the perspective of the seed to show its journey and the lifecycle of a plant.

Planning

Final piece of writing:

One September day I was happily sleeping in my seed pod. Then all of a sudden my pod opened and the wind picked me and my friends. Two of my friends got lost and one got stuck in a tree. Eventually I settled down on a freshly cut lawn. In the night I wriggled until I was nice and warm in the soil.

It's Winter now and its freezing cold. I really should get to sleep. Before I go to sleep my best friend got eaten by a very greedy rat. Luckily he missed me. I tucked up and eventually got to sleep. My last friend got dug up by a shovel but I stayed fast asleep.

Its getting warmer and I think it's spring. All my friends are germinating but not me. One of my friends started growing really close to a really big weed it blocked out all the sunlight and rain so he died. Eventually I germinated and my roots started to grow down and my shoots went up. My roots became anchored in the soil and my shoots are stretching up to the sun.

It's summer now and there are lots of other plants around. Look I've already got my big white and pink flower. Lots of birds, butterflies and bees gather round to see my huge flower.

Its getting cooler and the wind is getting stronger. It's September and my seed pod pops and all my seeds have blown out. The wind carried them away to find their own homes and to start the life cycle.

In this example, Asha, has shown understanding of the seasons, correctly used the term germinate and described this process identifying that the roots grow down and the shoots grow up. She has also shown understanding of what parts of the plant do and the conditions needed for plants to grow when the weed takes all the sunlight and water and the other plants die.

It would be interesting to ask Asha what she thinks the seed needed to germinate. Children often think that seeds need the same things as a plant (light, water and soil). Most seeds do not need light to germinate and as they contain a food and nutrient store they also do not require soil. This surprises children and it is a great enquiry: Do seeds need soil to germinate? Growing seeds in damp cotton wool or on a damp piece of kitchen roll allows the children to find out the answer to this question and also clearly observe what happens to the seed.

Year 4	
Topic	Solids, liquids and gases

After learning about solids, liquids and gases, changes of state and finally the water cycle children were asked to write a diary entry from the perspective of a water droplet.

A diary of a water droplet

Dear friends, you will not believe what has happened...
Whilst I was floating in a luxury outdoor swimming pool I suddenly began to evaporate. I

slowly raised up from the ground upwards and upwards. I'm on the top of the world I thought in a silly way. Suddenly I started getting really cool. No, no, no! Not the cool where you are totally awsome, well I am pretty awsome though. Well any way back to the story. So I was floating through the atmosphere when I began to cool down (condense). Bbbbbbrr it realy is cold I thought. Suddenly, I saw, no it couldn't be, could it. It was Sammy the squirrel and all the other water droplets. Just to note, Sammy is not a squirrel, he is obviously a water droplet, squirrels do not evaporate, don't try and make one evaporate or your parents won't cook dinner and you'll have to eat a squirly squirrel. I went over to Sammy and had a little chat. A while later, when we were talking about old songs and tunes. When we got to this part of (the part of) the piggy tune you know the one that goes wee, wee, wee all the way home as if by magic precipitation happened, but for us it was more like aaargh, aaargh, aaargh, all the way through the aaaargh tmosphere!!! We fell through the atmosphere in the form of water droplets as we fell I saw the sun and he had his hat on! When I finally stopped falling, I look around me and there was so much snow and ice. Wow, it was snow cold! Sorry, couldn't resist adding that part. Well, back once again back to our story. It was so freezing

Getting creative with
science recording

that I began to freeze, I looked all around
and was horrified by what I saw... All my
friends, all my family and even silly Sammy the
squirrel! P.S. He's obviously not a squirrel. They where
frozen. I looked at myself - aaaargh!
I was frozen solid too. It seemed like
months later, when I suddenly began to turn
back to liquid., I was free! My entire
family and friends too, we joined together
into one long stream. Sammy the non squirrel,
told me it was called collection. At the end
of the stream was my, my, my home! I was
so excited I was back - well for now that
is the end of our story, actually aaargh
good aaaargh bye I'm evaporating and
aaaargh arising.

It seems clear that Jake has become immersed
in the story writing. Although the science
terminology is hidden between the creative
additions, we can see that Jake has understood
the water cycle and the parts played by
evaporation and condensation. He has linked
temperature changes to condensation and
freezing. The next step, would be to talk to Jake
about how the temperature affects the rate of
evaporation. This might be an area he is not yet
secure on and the class could learn about this
through an enquiry into where the best place to
dry wet socks might be.

Other examples of where children could write recounts to share understanding:

- Journey of a sandwich to show understanding of digestion in Year 4

- Journey of a red blood cell to show understanding of the heart and circulatory system in Year 6

- Diary of an animal to explain the stages in its lifecycle in Year 5

- Diary of a tree throughout the seasons in Year 1

- Recount from the perspective of a raisin after observing dancing raisins (raisins in lemonade) in Year 4 solids, liquids and gases

- Recount from the perspective of a floating cotton wool ball (activity in part 1) in Year 1 materials

- Recount from a magnet rescuing keys from down a drain or paperclips from a cup of water in Year 3 forces and magnets

Getting creative with science recording

Documentaries and Script writing

There are now lots of science and nature documentaries that children may have watched at home or at least heard of. These are often presented by well- known TV personalities such as Sir David Attenborough. These could be used to inspire children to share their understanding in the form of a TV programme. Children could act these out and film them and/or write a script.

Year 6	
Topic	Evolution and Inheritance

Year 6 pupils enjoyed writing scripts and then acting them out in front of a green screen.

Hi, welcome back to the animal channel. Today we are in centeral Australia studying the thorny devil, one of Australia's most interesting animals. I am joined by scientist: and Explorer: who are going to answer some of my questions.

Hello, it's a pleasure to be here.

Thanks very much for having us.

My first question is for you, ~~Does~~ How does the thorny devil camuflage it's self in the wild?

Thats a good question. They ~~change~~ are coloured in shades of desert-browns and tans to blend into their backgrownd, when they're not changing colours. This is something that they do ~~in the~~ depending on the climate : in warm weather they are pale yellow, in old ~~they~~ they are dark colours.

Wow! Thats really interesting! Now, How big ~~are~~ can ~~they grow~~ the thorny devil grow?

although

Well, they only live for 15-20 years, they only grow to 20 centermetres. So to look bigger, they puff themselves out.

Really? My last question is: Do they have any other names?

Yes; it's scientific name: M'Moloch horridus'; 'horned lizard' and 'thorny toad.'

Thank you for watching the animal channel.

See you next time.

Goodbye!

> In this example, Amy has identified one adaptation that her imaginary animal has (it can camouflage). It is not clear why it does this e.g. to avoid predators or hide from prey. She has mentioned what could be inferred as another adaptation but has not described why it puffs up. To really show that she understands how animals are adapted to suit their environment she could be encouraged to add more detail.

Other examples of where children could use TV shows and scripts to show their understanding:

Children could interview a scientist to explain the results from a range of enquiries such as:

- How much sugar there is in our drinks? (Year 2 and Year 4)

- What does sugar do to the surface of egg shells (which is like our teeth enamel)? (Year 4)

- How does exercise affect the heart rate? (Year 6)

Getting creative with science recording

Newspaper report

There are lots of science discoveries which are shared in newspaper reports. This can be a great way for children to share their understanding as their newspaper reports briefly describe the investigation, give a conclusion and sometimes comment on how much the results should be trusted. They will also need to be entertaining for the reader.

Year 5	
Topic	Properties and changes of materials

The class had been learning about dissolving and had a good understanding of what the term meant. The children were challenged to come up with their own enquiry about dissolving based on what they had learnt so far. Each group had their own question which they investigated. The children were then asked to individually write about the findings from their enquiries in a newspaper report. They were given the task of making it appealing and interesting to the reader as well as linking it to real life.

Find Out What Sugar To Put In Your Drink

Have you ever wondered which is the best type of sugar to put in your coffee? Look no further. We have finally cracked the complicated case of dissolving.

Using their incredible intellect and investigative skills a group of young scientists set out to investigate: How does the type of sugar affect the number of stirs taken to dissolve?

The scientists began by conducting extensive market research to find out what types of sugar were available for sweetening hot drinks. From this, they then chose four types to test: granulated sugar, caster sugar, demerara sugar and cane sugar. The same amount, 1 teaspoom, of each sugar was added to 120ml of water in the same sized container.

The surprising results can be seen in the table below.

Caster sugar	5 stirs	8 stirs	7 stirs	Average= 7 stirs
Granulated sugar	9 stirs	9 stirs	11 stirs	Average= 10 stirs
Demerara Sugar	14 stirs	18 stirs	15 stirs	Average= 16 stirs
Cane sugar	10 stirs	12 stirs	11 stirs	Average= 11 stirs

The scientists found that caster sugar took the least amount of stirs at 7 stirs on average. This was under half the amount of the demerara sugar. Using their incredible brains the scientists worked out that this is because the grains of caster sugar are much smaller which makes it easier to dissolve.

The results were repeated to check that no mistakes were made in counting. Stirring in the same way was the most difficult part as the scientists admitted it was not easy to make sue the stirring was the same for all of the tests . Next time they also think they should make sure that all of the water is at exactly the same temperature.

So next time you are trying to decide what sugar to add to your hot drink think of these results. Find out more about the amazing world of science next week when we look at dissolving sweets.

In this example the enquiry question was: How does the type of sugar affect the number of stirs to dissolve?

In this example, Daniel, has shown an understanding of the need to control certain variables. His results are displayed clearly although there are no headings in his table. His has used the results to draw a correct conclusion and started to use the data to support his statement. He has also thought about why the caster sugar dissolved quicker.

Getting creative with science recording

In terms of an evaluation Daniel has pointed out an issue with stirring in the same way although he has not thought about he could improve the method to account for this. He has identified a variable, the temperature of water, which wasn't controlled that should have been. It would be good to talk to Daniel about why he thinks this needs to be controlled to check his understanding.

Overall, this is a great example of how children can be given an audience to write for and demonstrate development of key scientific skills and English skills. The class also really enjoyed sharing their findings in this way.

Note: when children are asked to explain why they need to control/ or keep something the same they often say to make it a fair test. A far better answer is to explain how not controlling that variable would affect their results. For example: *"Next time we should make sure the water we use is all at the same temperature because sugar dissolves quicker in hotter water so if the water was hotter for one of the sugars that would have made it dissolve quicker."*

Other contexts for using newspaper reports:

- The best value for money kitchen roll – following an enquiry into which kitchen roll is most absorbent in Year 2 materials

- The best value for money nappy – following an enquiry into the most absorbent nappy in Year 5 Properties and changes of materials

- The best exercise for raising heart rate – following an enquiry into exercise and pulse rate in Year 6 animals including humans

- The best shoes to wear in icy weather – following an enquiry into the force needed to move different shoes based on how much friction they create in Year 3 forces and magnets

- The best colour flowers for attracting bees
  (Children could write about this after conducting research or using the environment to complete a survey into the colour of flower and how many bees visit it in Year 3 plants.)

- The shocking findings about sugary drinks and how bad they are for teeth
  Year 4 – following testing egg shells in different sugary drinks

Letter writing

Children could be asked to share their understanding by writing a letter to a particular audience or character.

Year 2	
Topic	Uses of everyday materials – testing which material would be best for a shoe

The children in this class had been learning about materials and how to classify them according to properties and had begun to think about the best materials for different purposes. The class were set the challenge of finding out which material would be best to put on the teacher's son's shoes as he often slipped up. Each group felt and observed materials before attaching them to a shoe to test how easy or hard they were to pull. (The children did not use force meters to record the force needed to pull the shoe as this is more appropriate for the Year 3 Force topic).

Dear Miss Jackson,

We diskurved that all the matecals were good but there could only be one good material that was the best for your sons shoe and that was the sandpaper because it griped the best because it was rough. The hard rubber was really really bouncy and your son already has rubber on his show so ask him to put some sandpaper on his shoe.

From Stephanie

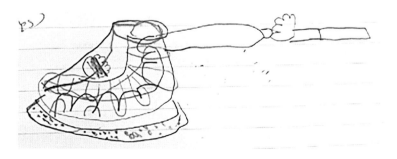

In this example, Stephanie has chosen a suitable material to solve the problem and used some vocabulary to describe the properties of the materials (rough and bouncy).

Year 5	
Topic	Properties and changes of materials

A mum from the school set the children in Year 5 the challenge of finding out what brand of nappy she should buy. The children in each group decided how they would know which was best and how to find out including how they should control variables that might affect their results. The children recorded their results in a results table and then wrote letters to the teacher to explain what they had found out.

Results:

Nappies	Dry	Wet	Dry	Wet
Pampers Baby Dry	28g	113g	27g	94g
Pampers Premium Protection	33g	145g	32g	118g
Little Angels comfort Dry	41g	123g	42g	119g
Little Angels Supreme Protection	38g	138g	38g	124g

Letter:

I am writing to you you about our science investigation that we carried out today. We tested the absorbency of of your different types of of nappies so we can let you know which type of nappie you should buy for your new baby. *A very good introduction!*

The four different nappies we tested are:

• Asda Little Angels Comfort Dry
• Asda Little Angels Supreme protection
• Pampers Baby Dry
• Pampers Premium Protection ✓

To keep our tests fair we used the same equipment and the same amount of water and we only had one variable. The one variable we had was the type of nappie we were testing. ✓

We carried out the test by first weighing the nappie when it was dry. Then we poured 150 ml into the nappie and weighed it. We did that for every nappie then double we did it again to see if we got reasonably the same results. ✓

The nappie I think is best is Pampers Premium Protection. I think this because it did not leek, it is very thick and soft and absorbed water in around 10-20 seconds. ✓ *It absorbed the most water.*

The things I think affected the investigation are when we were pouring water into the nappie it wasn't 150 ml. ✓

This letter shows that Jasmine has successfully identified and controlled variables that would have affected the results (how much water each brand of nappy absorbed). She has used observations to recommend a nappy based on the properties it would need although she did not actually make a conclusion based on her results. When prompted by the teacher she did also refer to the results to indicate that the Pampers Premium had absorbed the most water.

Jasmine has identified one error they may have made but not said how this might have affected the results or what they could do next time to improve this.

Getting creative with science recording

Other examples of where children could write letters to share their understanding:

- After investigating floating and sinking, a letter to the gingerbread man about what he could use as a raft to get across the river (instead of the fox) in Year 1 materials

- Before they start building their homes, a letter to the three pigs about the best material to use in Year 1 materials

- After studying the seasons throughout the year, a letter to Olaf from Frozen to explain what summer, spring and autumn are like and what he would need to be prepared

- A letter to other school children or parents about human's impact on the environment and what they can do in Year 4 living things and their habitat

- A letter to parents or other school children about what a healthy lunch box should contain in Year 2 animals including humans

Responding to letters

To give an enquiry a real-life context (like in the example from Jasmine) children could be given the task of responding to a letter from an individual or company who require help with a problem. For example, in Year 3 when learning about rocks children could be given this letter:

> Dear Year 3,
>
> I work for the local council and I would like to make a new statue for the local park. I have heard that you are learning about rocks and I would like you to find out what the best type of rock is for me to use.
>
> The rock for the statue will need to be strong and not easily breakable. Please bear in mind the statue will be outside so it will be rained on.
>
> Please test a range of rocks and write back with your recommendations.
>
> I look forward to hearing from you.
>
> Kind regards
>
> Mrs C. Smith

Getting creative with science recording

The children could then think about how to test a range of rocks, complete the investigation and finally write back. (Please note teachers could adapt this to name actual relevant parks or locations in the local community).

Head teachers can also write to children to set the scene for an enquiry for example:

Dear children,

I know that you are all fantastic scientists so I am coming to you for help.

I am fed up of dunking my biscuit in my tea at break and it falling to pieces in my cup. Can you please test a range of biscuits and find out which would be the best for dunking in tea so that I can change what I buy for the staff room.

Please work scientifically so that I can trust the results.

I look forward to hearing from you.

Kind regards

Mrs Smith

Getting creative with science recording

Instructions

Instructions are often seen in children's science books in the form of a method. This will sometimes tell us whether a child has thought about other variables that might affect their results and how they might control them.

Instructions can also be used to share and summarise what the children have learnt during one or more related enquiries. The examples below show how this has been achieved.

Year 3	
Topic	Light – instructions for making a shadow puppet

After learning about light sources and opaque, transparent and translucent materials, this class were challenged with making shadow puppets. They started by testing different materials to see which type of material made the darkest shadow. They practised making shadows with their hands and explored how to make a shadow bigger or smaller. They finally used all this learning to make shadow puppets for shadow puppet shows which they showed to the rest of the class. The teacher then asked them to write instructions for other children explaining how to make and use a shadow puppet.

How to make a shadow puppet

1. Get a opaque material. It has to be opaque as opaque materials block all of the light and make a darker shadow.
2. Cut the shape you want for your puppet out of your opaque material. stick your shape to a lollypop stick with sellotape. Now you can have fun with your puppet
3. Choose a good spot for your show. You will need a good light source like a torch, and a flat surface like a wall.
4. You can make the puppet look bigger and smaller. To make it look bigger move it closer to the light source.

> In this example, Liam, has shown understanding of the terms opaque and light source. He has used what he learnt from both enquiries to state that opaque materials make better shadows and that a shadow will look bigger if it is closer to the light source.

Getting creative with science recording

Year 4	
Topic	Sound – investigating cup phones

After exploring instruments and learning that sounds are made when something vibrates the children made cup phones and thought about things they could change to see if it affected how well they could hear the sound. Some groups tried using different types of cup, some groups looked at whether it worked if the string had knots and some groups looked at how long they could make the string. Each group shared what they had found out with the class and the children were asked to then summarise this by writing instructions for other children explaining how to make a cup phone.

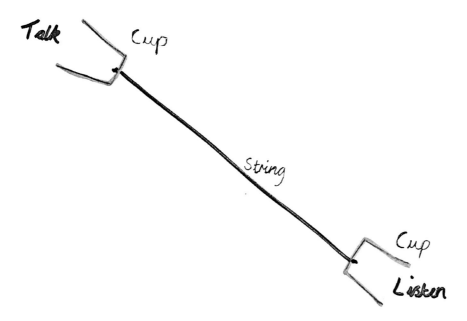

How to make a good cup phone (It's worth it. You will be amazed at how well they work)

1. You need two paper cups and a long piece if string with no knots. Paper cups work better than plastic.
2. Poke a hole in both of the bottom of the cups. Remember to ask an adult if you need help. Put the cups on the string and ties knots so they dont fall off.
3. Ask a friend to whisper in one cup and listen at the other end. You can swap afterwards.
4. It works best when the string is tight with no knots because the sound vibrations travels along the string
5. Try and find out how long you can make one. Our class made one that was 7 metres.

Other contexts where children could write instructions to share their understanding of:

- Looking after a plant in Year 2 or 3 plants

- Growing a plant from a seed in Year 2 plants

- Looking after a pet in Year 2 animals including humans

- Separating a mixture in Year 5 properties and changes of materials

- Making a periscope in Year 6 light

Using apps to help with recording and sharing understanding

Below are a list of apps that have been recommended by teachers for use in science to help children share their understanding.

Free apps

The Photos App. The built-in Photos app now allows the user to annotate photos and enhance them with filters etc. Children can use this app to label images etc. using the 'Markup' function.

Pic Collage. This allows children to make a collage of photos from the iPad. Add text and drawings. This image can then be saved, emailed or printed. Very easy to use.

Popplet Lite. This helps children capture and organise ideas in boxes. They can add photos, texts and diagrams and then save or email the output as a jpeg or pdf. This can be used to create mind maps or show the steps in an enquiry in a flow diagram.

Skitch. A tool for capturing and annotating images with text, arrows, shapes, emoticons and more.

Notes. The built-in Notes app now has a drawing / painting / whiteboard tool so that children can record and share their understanding. The finished work can be saved as an image to the camera roll and used in other apps.

Little Story Creator. A simple, free, digital book making app. Users can add images, text, stickers and voice-recordings to the pages of their books.

iMovie. Use this app to capture video and add text and more to the clips. You can also string together a series of still images and provide a recorded voice-over, to explain a process or the steps of an investigation.

Keynote. This is a presentations/slideshow creation app. Children can add text, images, videos and more to slides and present them as a slideshow.

iPad Screen Recording Function. From iOS11 it has been possible to record your on-screen actions to produce a video. This is great for explaining things. No extra apps are needed but the function does need to be enabled through the Control Centre settings in the Settings app. Once enabled, the user can use any app on the iPad, interact with the app and record what they are doing to produce a video. If you also want to record your voice, this needs to be enabled by holding down the screen-recording button in the Control Centre and then turning the microphone on.

Paid for apps

Green screen by Do Ink. This app uses the Chroma Key or Green Screen effect, which involves filming the subject in front of a green backing paper, cloth or painted wall. You can then layer this over a photo or video, so changing the background to anything you want. Great for getting children to narrate a nature documentary or space travel programme and teachers claim it is easy to use.

Book Creator. This allows the user to make digital books, with images, texts, pictures and video. Very easy to use and the books can be output in different formats such as ePub (an ebook,) PDF or video. Books can be emailed or printed, or read in iBooks.

Explain Everything. As the name suggests, this app is all about explaining, especially processes. It is a recordable whiteboard through which the user can record their voice while interacting with the whiteboard. All actions and movements on the board, along with the voice explanation, are recorded into a video.

There are many other apps available.

Important information. If you are using any app that requires a log-in and/or user accounts to be made, it is essential to review the privacy policy and terms/conditions of the app or service. Some such apps require users under 13 to have parental permission, for example. For data protection reasons, check with your Data Protection Officer (DPO) before using any service where data is being sent to a 3rd party.

Herts for Learning Ltd. has no affiliation with any company named in this information in any way. All product and company names are trademarks or registered trademarks of their respective holders. We evaluate the relevant apps that we mention but Herts for Learning Ltd. does not give approval or endorsement of those apps or services and we are not responsible for their content or accuracy.

Glossary

Accurate measurement:
To make an accurate measurement pupils need to use equipment properly to take careful measurements without error.

Control variable:
Variables that must be kept the same in a fair/comparative enquiry.

Dependent variable:
The variable that is measured to see how it changes in a fair/comparative enquiry.

Independent variable:
The one variable that is changed in a fair/ comparative enquiry.

Enquiry:
The process of asking scientific questions and finding answers through one of the five types of enquiry: fair/comparative testing, looking for a pattern, observing over time, identifying and classifying and research.

Fair test:
A type of enquiry which involves changing one variable to observe its effect while controlling all of the other variable.

Pattern seeking:
Observing and recording patterns in nature or carrying out a survey where all the variables cannot be controlled, e.g. proportions and ratios within the human body, which type of paper aeroplane flies further? (The last investigation question would be looking for a pattern not a fair test as it is not possible to control how hard it is thrown.)

Precise measurement:
To make a precise measurement pupils need to use measuring equipment with a smaller interval e.g. rulers in mm, temperature probes that measure to 0.1^0C and scales which measure to 1g etc.

Preliminary investigation:
A mini investigation carried out to work out how to run the full investigation.

Research:
Using books, the internet, pictures, visitors and experts as sources of evidence to answer questions.

Variable:
A factor that can be changed, controlled or measured in an investigation.